The Stopping Places

poems by

Amy L. George

Finishing Line Press
Georgetown, Kentucky

The Stopping Places

for Calvin, as always
and
in loving memory of Cathy Jean Kelly,
owner of Amsterdam Press
Thank you both for your faith in my words.

Copyright © 2018 by Amy L. George
ISBN 978-1-63534-456-1 First Edition
All rights reserved under International and Pan-American Copyright Conventions. No part of this book may be reproduced in any manner whatsoever without written permission from the publisher, except in the case of brief quotations embodied in critical articles and reviews.

ACKNOWLEDGMENTS

Thank you to the editors of the journals where the following poems first appeared:

Before the New Day—*Carcinogenic Poetry*
Before We Disappeared—*Poesia*
Burn the Chaff—*Red Ochre Press*
Compass—*The Rockett Review*
Ideogram—*Kyoto Journal*
The Mentor—*PoetsArtists*
The Reel World—*Words Dance*
Sayonara—*The Browsing Corner*
Sparrows—*letteR*
The Veteran—*Ouroboros Review*
Adopted; Tea for a Phoenix—*Pirene's Fountain*
Zen Garden—*Pirenes Fountain* and reprinted in *First Water: The Best of
    Pirene's Fountain*

The following poems first appeared in the chapbook *The Fragrance of Memory* (Amsterdam Press):

Focus
Memory (under the title Memory of Stones)
Morning Glory
Simplicity

Publisher: Leah Maines
Editor: Christen Kincaid
Cover Art: Sam Uglow
Author Photo: Andrea George
Cover Design: Elizabeth Maines McCleavy

Printed in the USA on acid-free paper.
Order online: www.finishinglinepress.com
         also available on amazon.com

Author inquiries and mail orders:
Finishing Line Press
P. O. Box 1626
Georgetown, Kentucky 40324
U. S. A.

Table of Contents

The Stopping Places

I. Spring

Turning 1
Adopted 2
Before the New Day 4
Simplicity 5
Fledgling 6
Compass 7

II. Summer

Morning Glory 10
Rowboat 12
Tea for a Phoenix 13
The Veteran 14
Zen Garden 15
Memory 16
Focus 17

III. Autumn

Burn the Chaff 20
Before We Disappeared 21
The Mentor 22
The Reel World 23
The Performance 24

IV. Winter

Linger 26
Sayonara 27
Propulsion 28
Ideogram 29
Sparrows 30

The Stopping Places

There's a road on every tombstone.

A journey is traced
in a single dash
from when light enters eyes
to the moment it leaves.

The length of the trip
doesn't matter as much
as the exits we take,
the shoulders we rest on,
the stars we gape at,
the hands we find to hold
at the stopping places.

It's at the stopping places
where our breath catches in our throats
at scenic overlooks, as we inhale
the wildness of the world,
drink in sights and faces
in the warmth of the sun,
and sometimes,
clutch each other tightly,
as we are drenched in rain.

The road winds
onward,
stretching out before us.

Best travel light while we can.

I. Spring

Turning

When the blossom is born,
it does not look to day of its death.

Rather, it looks to the sun's face,
the cool whisper of the river,

the turning of the wind
around its branches.

It looks to the blueness
of sky, water drops

of birdsong, falling to
dry earth.

The day's patina
burns orange.

Sky grows weary
of bearing the blossoms,

they fall,
but do not weep.

Adopted

I was small
when we left Korea,
the homeland
that only remembers me
as its acquaintance
and not as its child.
Memories
drift from forgotten places,
fan out before me
when I least expect them.

Fragrances remind me
of the pungent smell
of kimchi in pots
large enough to carry
small oceans,
or of gardens tended by women
on clay rooftops,
color bursting forth
as blossoms reached for the sun.

The homeless men downtown
wear the same eyes as street mermaids:
men whose legs
were encased in large rubber bags,
as they dragged themselves
along seas of black pavement,
singing mournfully,
sirens tempting men
to give up their gold.

Some days, the memories
come in flashes:
photographs
whose edges faded
with time.

There's a bar of
green soap,
an old Korean woman
washing me, chattering,
even though I don't understand.

Maybe she was scouring her own memories.

Before the New Day

The night crept over the edges
of the earth, became a silk sheet
tossed into the sky
as we sat in the shadow of a chapel
dreaming pinpoint star dreams.

The gypsy wind murmured in my ear
of faith in darkness.
Lady Moon held her position
while small streaks of fire
circled her, danced in her room,
her children celebrating
the end of the day.

Two clouds embraced each other,
held us in their grasp.

One bore your name
and the other, mine.

They drifted near,
then together, all of us
paused, clutching unspoken
desire for the night,
the warm blanket ache of shadow,
the joy of faithful light.

Simplicity

I miss the slower days
before adulthood settled into my bones.

My friends and I
waded out into the local river,
all of us shivering and laughing
at each other as we slipped
on the smooth rocks,
plunged waist deep
unexpectedly,
water splashing shocked faces.

A kayaker,
his craft pulled onto a boulder
in the middle of the current,
lay in the sun, eyes closed,
hands clasped behind his head.

We sloshed by near the shore,
joked about waking him.

Eventually, we headed back
to our cars, everyone's hair
dripping wet.

Life was nearer than death then.
And we were not afraid
to grasp it eagerly in our palms,
drink deeply from its depths.

Fledgling

Funny how our lives
hum the same tune, circularly,
pattern woven, ties restitched

until the atmosphere shifts and

someone or something
tears us from the comfort
of what we've always known

absence or presence,
ambition or mediocrity,
Pride or its brother, Fall.

Funny how, when the world
becomes a bigger place,
even the mirror enlarges itself.

And though we may not realize it,
our shadow becomes that of a giant's,
and the echo of our steps

reverberate louder,

even across days
weeks...
oceans.

Compass

In my mind,

you are fresh-faced and smiling,
in a land across a fickle sea,
where waves fail to mark time
in watery increments,
drowning minutes without mercy.

Before we realize it,
sunset is upon us
before our hands can meet again.

Tonight, I held your picture
in the moonlight,
and was reminded

of the tender sound
of water lilies,
breaking open,
faces to the sun,
bursting into bloom.

I will always think of you as
spring and lilting rain,
as all things new and

waters uncharted.

II. Summer

Morning Glory

I crept from the cabin
before the sun was awake.

The old stairs creaked
as I tiptoed down them,

groaned about the early hour,
and the dampness of the dew.

Crickets' songs
pierced the still-dark sky.

The water lapped against
the weathered pier,

and a fish leapt to taunt
any would-be fishermen.

I settled down on the floating dock,
crossed my legs underneath me,

and then she came,
blushing at first,

as if the whole world
had not waited on her.

Dawn stretched her arms
over the water, spread them

like a fire in the night,
banished the moon to his repose.

Her fingers reached to the blackbirds
and the windows of that sleepy cabin,

anointed my head,
and bathed my face

as the tresses of her hair
fell across the trees.

Rowboat

Loosing the boat from the dock,
we spoke of sanctuary.
The two oars became wings,
carried us out, away from
the weight of the earth.

You rowed gently,
paddles slicing the water,
water slicing the silence,
disturbing fish
and reflections of clouds.

Frogs clicked
occasionally and cicadas
hummed, their volume
rising and falling, rippling
out over the lake.

A heron glided overhead,
wings outstretched.
For a split second,
she shadowed our skiff,
a blue gray angel to bless us.

Tea for a Phoenix

On a scorched roadside
blanketed in billows of dust,
I met you again,
surrounded by weary pilgrims
heading to the temple.

Thirty summers had passed between us.
Your black hair had become woven
with strands of silver
as if heaven's clouds
had anointed your head.

We slipped inside a small room,
where a young man who could
have passed for your deceased son
served us steaming cups
of masala chai.

It tasted as it had
thirty years earlier...
the reviving spice of earth and stars,
fire and ginger,
soothed by moonlight and milk.

And I smiled to watch the steam
erase the lines
from your face,
unravel the resurrected Lazarus
of your youth.

The Veteran

Mr. Waters comes in
like the morning fog
each day,
drifts through my office door,
looking for a cup of coffee.

His voice echoes thunder left
over from some storm
that drenched a rice paddy
in Vietnam,
rain still falling behind dry eyes.

In a few moments, he will go to
his kitchen here at the facility,
prepare eggs and grits for
juveniles with gang
affiliations, drug charges.

None of these cocky boys
know this cook has killed
a man with his hands,
knows about death
as some of them do.

He shuffles to the door,
thunder fading,
past hanging out
of his back pocket,
dragging along the floor.

Zen Garden

In the center of a city
burning with the midday sun,

a garden,
a strange drop of calm

nourished my love and me,
sheltered us from the reach of chaos.

Lotus blossoms guarded silence,
only allowing dragonflies to whir through the emptiness.

Spiders spun their fragile dreams
as we wove our own through each other's fingers.

The pagoda alone heard us free our thoughts,
let them slip through flowered lips.

Shimmering koi watched them
course down the waterfalls and over stones,

swam beside them, a series of unbroken days
and promises not yet spoken.

Memory

I think of you
when I pour my cup of coffee
in the morning.
My coworker yawns
while the deejay on her radio
rumbles and rattles on
about celebrity divorce
and who got caught
driving drunk.

I find you in a quiet place,
a memory of stones
by the sea,
rocks we skipped
off of the breakwater
as the wind whipped
around us.
I remember the scent
of the salt,

the sound of seagulls
crying as they wheeled
through cloudy portals,
the breathing of the waves
thrashing against
the stone, and
the sound of our rocks
breaking the water,
plunging into the depths.

Focus

On certain days
when the earth
turns too quickly,
      I crave the wind.

I lie in the grass,
spread my arms like sails
let the migrant wind
      embrace me.

The fragrance of the woods
surges over my body,
pours over my face,
      swells in my lungs.

I forget the sound of the clock
ticking in its impatience,
and remember the cardinal truth:
      all action follows breath.

III. Autumn

Burn the Chaff

Break me down into particles, love...
minutia of breath and being...
remind me how to feels to run
barefoot down a dirt road
on an autumn day
when all the trees do is
burn, burn, shake and burn
just because they can.

Take my hand as we escape
this wreck of expectations,
finding answers under the stars of God.
The right words will be right behind us;
those fine, perfect words everyone wanted
us to say...followed by embers of
the box they wanted us to buy
to house our vagrant spirits.

Let's settle on the edge of the world.
Forget the fine china,
advice like bitter elixir,
gaping mouths, never satiated,
clothes we're supposed to crave.
I want to drink you in,
feel you like a secret against my lips,
remember the truth

that we are but dust.

Before We Disappeared

Some evenings when the wind
blows leaves across my path,
I remember how it felt...

The night whipped around us in that sliver
of eternity.
You wrapped me in your jacket,
whispered secrets until they fell into my hands,
burning softly,
the color of the moon in your eyes.

Morning came, and each star vanished.
We vanished, too.

Still
I sometimes think of how beautiful it was
to shiver with you under that October sky,
like the trembling of cherry blossom petals
before they fall.

The Mentor

His touch on her thoughts was art.
His experience sculpted her youth,

transformed dirt into monuments
on days they sat

across from each other
at the museum café

with coffee cups
and lined notebooks

in that northern city
that lacked enough color in the summer

and sunk back
into black and white each winter.

The Reel World

If I could,
I would rewind my life.

I would go back through all
the plot twists and turns

if only to be able to relive
that one beautiful moment:

The single scene to ensure your name
in the credits

even if I knew
in God's cutting room

the outcome of the film
wouldn't rely on its existence

at all.

The Performance

I watched a leaf fall this evening.
It floated back and forth as it descended,

conducted at the tip
of an invisible baton.

It landed with a quiet bow
and trees ceased applauding,

but the sky called it up again,
demanded an encore—

a whirling crescendo—
a dance across a blank stage.

The small dancer
obliged the wind,

as if knowing
it was entertaining me

in the final moments of light
before the dark curtain fell.

IV. Winter

Linger

The scent drifts by
turns my head as it descends,
drapes itself around my shoulders,
prods my mind with its tendrils.

A quiet fog disturbs the waters
the potent ache of smoke, spice,
honeyed promises...
you.
The world around me is hushed

a pause in the stillness
until time and wind
carry your memory off
into the past
the folding embrace of night.

Sayonara

That day at the art festival
the trees gave no hint that I would

catch a glance of you across the courtyard
behind the geisha with the painted smile.

She danced in front of our eyes like light.
Your gaze met mine, belying hours passed alone.

I remembered you adorning me with blossoms
before spring gave way to summer,

fall, winter snows that covered
every trace of your footprints.

You looked my way once more
and then, not again as the notes faded.

Time to let the blossoms fall,
blow away where they will.

If I were Picasso, I would paint love
in tight red circles,

silken lines like thread
from tattered kimonos.

Propulsion
    (in memory of those who've slipped away)

Memories of you
fall
through my mind,
settle in my heart, and
the pit of my stomach.

Your absence has transformed me.

Like blood rushing
through me,
pulsating,
life-giving,

the tone of your voice,
the look in your eyes,
your open hands,
your particular mannerisms

reverberate again inside of me.

I breathe deeply,
then carry on, move forward,
pushed by your gentle goading

to live my own life,

in moving tribute to us both.

Ideogram

To teach me our mother tongue,
language of brush and ink,
you placed your hand over mine.

I believed in the travel of the lines,
each stroke a beggar without his brother,
up, down,
circle,
solitude, joining,
now love,
now tears.

I watched a single swoop
become a flock of birds
taking wing near the moon
imagined them cutting across the sky,
tearing through the temple garden of stars.

I paid attention to the correct way
to paint the sound of journeys,
the wind wrapping itself around bamboo.

Because of your hands,
I learned how to paint *joy,*
rest, serenity…
and when the time came,

farewell.

Sparrows

As the snow starts to fall
I look outside my window
and shiver as I stare
at the solid curtain sky.
Sparrows fly for shelter,
flutter to the ground,
hop under my berry bushes,
all powdered and sprinkled
with frost,
fluffing out tiny bodies
with trembling wings.
I pity them, out in the elements,
until I notice
they are peeking at each other
from under their leafy tents,
flitting back and forth,
chattering like children
at play, altogether
undeterred by the cold.

Amy L. George is the author of two other poetry chapbooks, *Desideratum* (Finishing Line Press) and *The Fragrance of Memory* (Amsterdam Press), as well as a small collection entitled *Sacred Fire and Ebullient Flames* (Red Ochre Press). Her poetry has been published in various journals, such as *Kyoto Journal, Toronto Quarterly, Pennsylvania English, Pirene's Fountain, Up the Staircase, PoetsArtists, MIPOesias,* and others.

Her poetry has also appeared in the following anthologies: *First Water: The Best of Pirene's Fountain* (Glass Lyre Press), *Sing Now, America!* Anthology (Virgogray Press), and *The Working Poet: 75 Writing Exercises and an Anthology* (Autumn House Press). Her poem "Among Us" appears in *Not Yet Christmas: It's Time for Advent—A Daily Reader* (Seedbed).

She holds an MFA in Creative Writing from National University where she served as a student poetry editor for The GNU, the literary journal of National University, during her time as a graduate student.

After completing her MFA, she edited and published a bi-annual online journal of narrative poetry called *Bird's Eye reView* from 2008–2012.

An English instructor, she teaches courses in fiction and poetry at Southwestern Assemblies of God University and is currently pursuing her Ph.D. in Literature and Criticism.

She lives in Waxahachie, Texas with her husband and their three feline divas.

www.ingramcontent.com/pod-product-compliance
Lightning Source LLC
LaVergne TN
LVHW041504070426
835507LV00012B/1314